HOW TO READ THE BIBLE
Building Skills for Bible Study

ISBN 978-1-949628-14-2
Printed in the United States of America.
10 9 8 7 6 5 4 3 2 1   22 21 20 19

Published by The Pastoral Center, http://pastoral.center.

Developed in partnership with MennoMedia and Brethren Press. Series editors: Fumiaki Tosu, Ann Naffziger, and Paul Canavese. *How to Read the Bible:* Writer: David Schroeder. Project editor, Lani Wright. Staff editors, Susan E. Janzen, Julie Garber, and James Deaton. Updated design, Paul Stocksdale.

All rights reserved. Purchase of this book includes a license to reproduce this resource for use in a single parish, school, or other similar organization. You are allowed to share and make unlimited copies only for use within the organization that licensed it. If you serve more than one organization, each should purchase its own license. You may not post this document to any web site without explicit permission to do so. Outside of these conditions, no part of this book may be reproduced in any form or by any means, electronic or mechanical, including photocopying, recording, taping, or via any retrieval system, without the written permission of The Pastoral Center, 1212 Versailles Ave., Alameda, CA 94501. Thank you for cooperating with our honor system regarding our licenses.

For questions or to order additional copies or licenses, please call 1-844-727-8672 or visit http://pastoral.center.

Portions of this work © 2019 by The Pastoral Center / PastoralCenter.com. Adapted and published with permission from Generation Why Bible Studies. © 1996, 2014 Brethren Press, Elgin, IL 60120 and MennoMedia, Harrisonburg, VA 22803, U.S.A. All rights reserved.

Unless otherwise noted, the Scripture passages contained herein are from the *New Revised Standard Version of the Bible*, copyright © 1989 by the National Council of the Churches of Christ in the United States of America. Used by permission. All rights reserved.

Bible-based Explorations of Issues Facing Youth

» OVERVIEW

When conversing online, the acronym IRL stands for "in real life." The virtual world of social media, text chats, blogs, and more have the power to remove us from the real world. What we experience online can skew our perspective on what it means to be human. It can numb us, incite us, distract us, depress us, confuse us, and make us rude or impatient. Strangely, this supposedly "social" and "connected" technology can profoundly disconnect us from others.

Religious faith can also place us in a bubble, especially when it distances us from others. When we keep the prophetic message at a safe distance, obscured in theological language and abstractions, we are missing the whole point. And when we see our parish as an insider club that serves itself, we can forget the radically inclusive message entrusted to us: God's love is for *everyone*, and God expects us to transform the *whole world* through that love.

Through the incarnation, God showed up in the real world to show us that our faith is not just about talking the talk, but also walking the walk. It can be risky. It can be confusing. It can hurt. But living out our faith can also bring us great purpose, peace, and joy.

This series connects the Bible with the tough questions that youth (and adults) encounter in their neighborhood, in school, among friends, and even online. This process will help you as a leader break open these issues in a fun and meaningful way, sparking conversation and the kind of life change Jesus invites us to embrace.

» THE ROLE OF PARENTS

As children enter middle school and high school, they become more independent, self-reliant, and, well, self-centered. This can bring parents to make assumptions that this is the time to step back, giving their child more space to form their identity. While there is truth to that at some level (adolescents definitely shouldn't be smothered), this is a stage of life when parents should in fact *lean in*. The apparent confidence and bluster youth show on the outside can mask the insecurity and confusion on the inside. Youth need their parents to be involved more than ever.

» WHOLE FAMILY FORMATION

Parents are the primary teachers of their own children, and parishes are waking up to the fact that faith formation programs need to bring parents into the process if they hope to see faith passed on to the next generation. Recent studies give us more and more evidence that the role of parents is the most important factor in determining whether a child will embrace faith as they move toward adulthood. Research from the Center for the Applied Research on the Apostolate shows that parents who talk about their faith and show through their actions that their faith is important to them are more likely to have children who remain Catholic.

More about Whole Family Formation >>>

To learn more about how your parish can take a comprehensive whole family approach to faith formation, visit **GrowingUpCatholic.com**.

While whole family events with elementary-aged children are on the rise, the role of parents can be an afterthought in youth ministry. We have designed the sessions in this series to work with or without parents present, and we encourage you to offer them as parent-child events.

If you choose to involve parents, it is important to consider before each session how to best do so. Many of the activities in this series are high-energy, creative, or silly. Some parents may need some encouragement to get out of their heads and have fun with the group. A few activities involving physical contact would be inappropriate for parents and youth to participate together, and we have noted them as such.

There are a number of ways to approach discussions with parent participation. Unless you have a small group, you will likely want to break into smaller groups for conversation. Some youth may be self-conscious and unable to be completely honest and open in a group situation with a parent present. For this reason, you may choose in some cases to assign parents to different groups from their own children, or to have separate parent and child groups altogether. Be sure to cover expectations around confidentiality. It is inappropriate for a parent (or youth) to share with another parent what their child said in a small group.

Note that even if parents and their children do not share all conversations together in the session, they will still have a valuable shared experience and can have extended conversations about it later.

>> **THANK YOU**

The role you play in gathering, animating, praying with, and forming youth is a valuable one. Thank you for all you do to serve the church and its families!

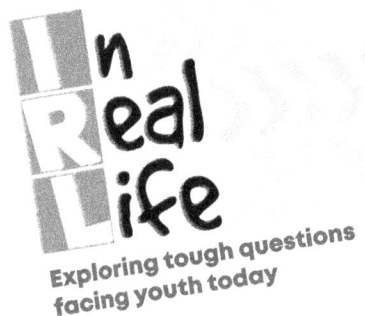

Bible-based Explorations of Issues Facing Youth

HOW TO READ THE BIBLE
Building Skills for Bible Study

>> INTRODUCTION

Do you feel as though you've inherited one of the downswings of the Bible literacy pendulum? Why don't people, particularly youth, read this wonderful resource called the Bible? You start with Genesis 1, with great intentions, and quickly get bogged down in genealogies and technical legalities. You get *bored*. So how can we read the Bible and fall in love with it?

One of the best things Bible study leaders can do is let their own love of the Bible *show*. That kind of love is contagious. Then start with the important things like, What does the Bible tell us about God? How did the Bible come to be? How did God communicate with people before there was a Bible? Who wrote it? Where did it come from and where will it lead us? What does God expect from us? What does it have to say to us today?

The Catholic take on the Bible is summarized in an important document from the Second Vatican Council called *Dei Verbum*, also known as the *Dogmatic Constitution on Divine Revelation*. In this document, the bishops teach that the Bible is one of many ways God has been communicating who God is to us. In fact, God has been trying to share this with us since the beginning of time—through creation itself, then through specific individuals like Abraham, Sarah, Moses, Miriam, and the other prophets. This revelation of God is then perfected in the words and actions of God's Son, Jesus (*Dogmatic Constitution on Divine Revelation*, 3-4).

The Bible represents the part of revelation that was written down—the stories the people of God considered most sacred and important to pass on. However, it is important to remember that revelation came first, before it was written down as Sacred Scripture, and that not *all* revelation was written down. Some of it was handed down to us through the life, worship, and oral traditions of the people of God, and we call that Sacred Tradition. In the Catholic faith, Sacred Scripture and Sacred Tradition are two especially important sources of revelation. The one can't exist without the other, and they both have the same origin—God (*Dogmatic Constitution on Divine Revelation*, 9).

We also need to remember not to make either the Bible or Tradition into an idol. Both point us to God, but they are *not* God. While they can draw us closer to God, they should never be the object of our worship.

>>

"[T]here exists a close connection and communion between sacred tradition and Sacred Scripture. For both of them, flowing from the same divine wellspring, in a certain way merge into a unity and tend toward the same end."

Dogmatic Constitution on Divine Revelation, 9.

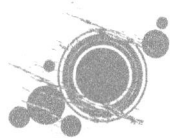

⟩⟩⟩ EXTENDER SESSION

Extender sessions suggest special activities related to the issue of the unit. They help accommodate the diversity of parish schedules. Since each unit is undated, participants may study units in their entirety and still participate in special events of the parish that get scheduled simultaneously with youth group time. Extender sessions can be used anytime, but the one for this unit best follows **Session 5**. Calculate now whether or not you will be using the extender session, and when.

In this series, we will focus on helping participants learn to read, love, and draw inspiration from Scripture. As Christians and as leaders, we want to pass on the life-giving and life-shaping stories of the Bible. Even better is to offer to young people the tools for delving into that rich storehouse of faith, so that they do not have to depend on someone else for knowledge and decision-making about the Bible, like people did before literacy was available to "common people."

The goal of this unit is to help participants find their way through the Bible and make it an effective study tool for their life of faith. The unit includes resources that help participants study the Bible and understand the context in which the stories were handed down. What it *can't* necessarily convey is a love of the Bible and a relationship to the God toward whom it points. That's *your* job. But you don't have to do it alone. Ask the Spirit to help you!

⟩⟩ PREPARATION ALERT

Some of the participants in your group may have been given Bibles when they were in grade school. They're probably ready for a different kind of Bible now, one with study aids that will help them dig deeper. Consider getting youth to "own" their Bibles by pairing them up with adults who will shop with them for a study Bible. Perhaps you can get your congregation to foot the bill. This activity is the crux of the Extender Session. Feel free, however, to go on the Bible-buying spree *before* you start the unit, if you want participants to learn by using their own Bibles throughout this study.

The study also makes use of a number of Bible study helps, such as concordances, commentaries, study Bibles, and Bible dictionaries. Gather as many of these as you can find, and create a temporary "library" of Bible study resources to have on hand throughout the course. You can find a good selection at http://pastoral.center/scripture-reference.

THE TEACHING PLAN: The parts of the session guide

⟩⟩ **Faith story.** The session is rooted in this Bible passage.

⟩⟩ **Faith focus.** This is the story of the passage in a nutshell.

⟩⟩ **Session goal.** The entire session is built around this goal. What changes—in knowledge, attitude, and/or action—do you desire in your group?

⟩⟩ **Bible study skills to be practiced in this session.** This focuses on the tools and resources needed for in-depth Bible study.

⟩⟩ **Materials needed and advance preparation.** This is what you will need if the session is to go smoothly. You'll feel more at ease if you've taken care of these details before you meet your group.

⟩⟩ FROM LIFE TO BIBLE TO LIFE

The teaching plan we use is called *life-centered*. However, when we write each session, we always begin with Scripture. We ask, what does this particular passage say, especially to youth? Each session moves from life to Bible to life. So the Bible is really at the center of this way of teaching.

In every session we try to hit upon a tough question that participants might ask. Find out what questions on this issue are important for your group. Feel free to bring your own input and invite your group members to add their own experiences.

TEACHING THE SESSION

The five step-by-step movements will carry you from *life to the Bible and back to life*. Each session takes about 45 to 50 minutes. If there is a handout sheet for the session, take note of any complementary activities and stories.

1. **Focus.** This activity is intended to create a friendly climate within the group and to draw attention to the issue.
2. **Connect.** Talking, drawing, role playing, and other activities invite participants to express their own life experiences about the issue. Also use memory, reason, or imagination to get the group thinking about *why* they view the issue the way they do.
3. **Explore the Bible.** With a minimum of lecturing, dig into the faith story and search for answers to questions raised in the first activities. The Insights from Scripture section will help clarify the faith story. Help participants discover how the faith community understands the Bible passage.
4. **Apply** the faith story. This is the "aha!" moment when participants realize the faith story has wisdom for their lives.
5. **Respond.** What will the group do about the issue in light of what they have learned from their own experiences set alongside the faith story? At this point, the faith story becomes lived rather than a mere intellectual exercise.

LOOK AHEAD

Here are reminders for what you need to do for the next session or two.

INSIGHTS FROM SCRIPTURE

Here is a resource for Explore the Bible. Don't try to use all the material given. Take what you need to lead the session and answer questions your group may have. Let the Insights section inspire you to think and study more about the passage for the session.

HANDOUT SHEETS

Occasionally, there will be a handout sheet to complement your session. If you choose to use this, you will need to make enough copies for the group. These sheets may include questions, stories, agree/disagree exercises, charts, pictures, and other materials to stimulate your group to think and discuss.

Generally, no participant preparation is required unless the session plan calls for you to contact selected group members for specific tasks.

> "You forget your mobile phone – oh! I do not have it, I go back to look for it... What would happen if we treated the Bible like we treat our cell phone? Think about this. The Bible always with us, close to us."
>
> Pope Francis

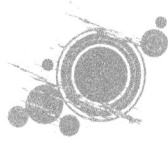

>>> **SESSION 1**

WHEN THERE WAS NO BIBLE >>>
The Bible as Revelation

Exploring tough questions facing youth today

>>> KEY VERSE

"I will make of you a great nation, and I will bless you, and make your name great, so that you will be a blessing." (Genesis 12:2)

>>> FAITH STORY

Genesis 12:1-7; 15:18-20; 17:15-22

>>> FAITH FOCUS

This is the story of how Abraham and Sarah became aware of God and God's promise. Even before there was a Bible, Abraham and Sarah came to know God because they responded to God's promises in faith and trust. Thus, beginning with Abraham and Sarah, a people with no Bible came to know God. Eventually, people wrote about their experience of God's revelation. Some of those stories became the Bible. Though the story of Abraham and Sarah is ancient history, God is interested in communicating with us at all times. It's up to us to be open to hear and respond to God.

>>> SESSION GOAL

Help participants see how the Bible is a people's testimony of how they experienced God and how God's character and will were first revealed because God made and kept promises.

>>> Materials needed and advance preparation

- Writing paper
- Antique tool or kitchen implement (could even be an invention of your own, the use of which is not readily recognizable)
- Bibles
- Four drinking glasses and three table knives (*Option A* in Apply). Fill one of the glasses with water. Practice the stunt ahead of time.
- Chalkboard/chalk or newsprint/marker
- Copies of the handout sheet for Session 1

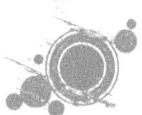

TEACHING PLAN

1. FOCUS 5 minutes

Put an antique tool or kitchen implement, something youth would not likely recognize, on a table in the middle of the room. Let people look at it, handle it, wonder about it. Ask, *What do you think it's used for? What might you call it? How could we find out about it?* (If someone *does* know what it's for, ask them to imagine that they don't know what it is, and think of other uses or meanings for it.) The point is to get people thinking about how they get familiar with an unfamiliar object.

2. CONNECT 5-10 minutes

Now move from getting to know the *object* to the *people* in your group. Have each person tell something about themselves that others do not know. It could be a hobby or special interest or special dream or something they have done. The idea is not to share some deep secret, but simply some information. Start the process by sharing something about yourself. Keep it short by restricting stories to 25 words or less.

Then pick up the antique and say, *It's easy to get to know **things**. You see, touch, smell, taste, or hear them. But how do you come to know a **person**? What do you think?*

You will probably get responses phrased in terms of what people *said* and *did*. Point out how each of the responses show up things that *reveal who the person is*. **We know a person through self-revelation!** Make this point.

But there is something missing. A person may be known differently by two different people, even if they've heard and seen the same things. Why? In order for us to know a person there has to be self-disclosure (revelation) from the person we are learning to know, and we have to respond appropriately to that revelation.

Now help the group take the next step. Ask: *How do we learn to know God? Imagine there are people who know nothing about God. They have no Bible. There is no one to tell about God. How can God connect with such people?* Ask for suggestions.

Participants may say "God spoke to them" through a dream or some critical event. But regardless of the means through which it is suggested that God was revealed, ask how they know it to be true. Is it more than wishful thinking or inherited belief?

Shift to the next activity by saying: *Of course, there really was a time when there was no Bible, and no one to tell about God. Abraham and Sarah and their people lived at such a time. But the way they came to know God is the way we can come to know God. Let's see what happened.*

3. EXPLORE THE BIBLE 25 minutes

Divide into three groups. Assign one of the following Bible passages to each group:

- Genesis 12:1-7
- Genesis 15:18-20
- Genesis 17:15-22

Ask each group to identify the promise God made to Abram and Sarai. After a few minutes, have them **identify the promise** of their passage with the larger group. (Make sure participants are not confused by the names Abram/Abraham and Sarai/Sarah—see Genesis 17:5, 15).

Then give the following mini-lecture. Write the main headings on the chalkboard or newsprint.

The setting
Abram and Sarai and their people left their homeland in Ur of the Chaldeans. It could have been because of war or famine; we are not told. We know that Abram and Sarai were concerned about the life of their people. Where should they graze the cattle? How could they survive without land?

God is present to Abraham
God came to Abraham in this crisis with the promise of life. It was a promise, and there were as yet no guarantees. It could have been a subjective, inner feeling on

the part of Abraham for he did not yet know that God would keep the promise. But Abraham became aware of God's presence with him and he received the word of promise.

God's promise
God's promise was related to Abraham and Sarah's deepest concerns. Their first concern was about being able to survive as a people. God promised that they would become a great people! They had no land and God promised them land! Abraham and Sarah had no son to inherit their property and people, and God gave them a son. The promises all related to their need. It was almost too good to believe.

The response of Abraham and Sarah
Abraham and Sarah believed in and accepted God's message as a promise of life. Maybe they felt they didn't have any better prospects! At any rate, they staked their lives and that of the people on the promise. They acted on it.

The confirmation of the promise
Even though it wasn't always easy to "keep the faith," Abraham and Sarah eventually realized that God had indeed kept the promise of life. God protected them on their journey. They came to no harm though they were in enemy territory. God gave Abraham and Sarah a son. At the end of Sarah's life, Abraham managed to buy the cave of Macpellah and took this as a sign that the land would someday belong to his people.

By believing and responding to God's promises, Abraham and Sarah learned that God is faithful. They might have been going out on a limb to believe in the first place, because they had little to go on. But eventually, the evidence piled up: God makes promises full of life, and keeps them.

Witness to the revelation received
This confirmed promise had to be shared with others, and what they shared became the basis of other people's faith and trust in God. As more and more people confirmed the truth of God's promise, it became important to remember what God had done for the people. It was so important that it became a sacred trust.

4. APPLY 8 minutes

Option A: Put participants in the place of Abraham and Sarah, the ones who learn to trust the promise, by doing the following stunt:

Place three glasses on a table in a triangle a little longer than a knife-long span away from each other. Say:

I plan to support the fourth glass, full of water, in the middle of the other glasses at glass--height above the table, using the three knives. Who believes I can do it? (Wait for response.) *Who is willing to take off their shoe and put it in the middle of the glasses,* **under** *the full glass of water? I promise I won't get it wet.*

Weave the knives as shown, and the support you create will hold the fourth glass easily.

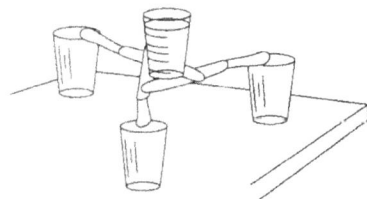

Go on to *Option A* in Respond.

LOOK AHEAD

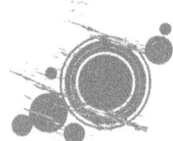

Keep adding to your "library" of Bible study resources for this unit: Have study Bibles and concordances on hand for the next session. A digital camera or phone camera is also called for in one option.

>>>

The Bible is actually a "library" of 73 books (66 for Protestants) written over a span of more than 1000 years. What ties these books together, says Bible scholar Etienne Charpentier, is that they are written by people "seized with a passion for God."

>> **Option B:** Put participants in the place of the promise-maker. Say: *Like God before the Bible, you as a worker don't have much written work history to recommend you to a potential employer. How do you get an employer to take you when you have no experience?*

Distribute handout sheets ("Job Recommendation"), and ask everyone to think of their dream job. How would they get someone to believe they could do it? Then divide the group into pairs to role-play a job interview. One person will be the job seeker, the other the employer. The job seeker has two minutes to convince the employer to take them on, and the employer should take written notes on the back of the handout sheet during the two minutes. (If participants have trouble getting started, suggest these things for convincing the employer: *Who can verify that you are trustworthy? References? What have you done in the past? What do you promise for the future? What assurances can you give?*)

After the two minutes, switch roles, so everyone gets a chance as employer.

Go on to *Option B* in Respond.

5. RESPOND 5 minutes

>> **Option A:** Distribute paper and pencils, and ask everyone to **leave some kind of record** of what happened here. *What will you tell about the event of the amazing knives? What will you tell about the leader who did this?* (Though it may look like you as leader are fishing for compliments, the point is to show that you kept a promise to do something that looked as if it couldn't be done.) When participants write down the story of how that promise was kept, they are leaving a record just as those who wrote down the events in the Bible left a record of how God keeps promises.

Close with prayer, thanking God for communicating with us, and asking for ears to be open to the message of love and care and promise. Then leave the "records" in the room, posting them on walls or on the chalkboard, so they will be reminded at the next session what happened.

>> **Option B:** Have everyone think back to their role as employer, or even use the notes they took. On the front of the handout sheet, each person should write a job recommendation for their partner, using the questions on the sheet.

Sharing the recommendations will also be a way of affirming each other. Then point out that the Bible is like a letter of recommendation—a people's testimony of how they experienced God and how God was revealed through promises made, and kept.

Suggested benediction: *God blesses us by keeping promises. Go and tell others.*

INSIGHTS FROM SCRIPTURE

REVELATION IS PRIOR TO SCRIPTURE

Scripture is *about* revelation and comes *from* revelation. The Bible shows us that God wants to communicate with us, wants to have a relationship with us. It is not primarily a rule book, but a book telling us about who God is and about God's vision for us. But God is never fully disclosed, and God can communicate even without a book, and did so before there was a Bible.

The Bible came into being as a result of revelations received from God over many years. Yet we can hardly imagine a time when there was no Bible that told us about God. We have the idea that our knowledge of God came from the Scriptures, and it does in a sense, but originally the Scriptures came from the revelations of God to people in various times and places. In other words, the story of how we got the Bible begins with Abraham and Sarah, those to whom God was first revealed, rather than with the creation stories. Writing down the *experience* of God came after the realization that there *was* a God who made promises and kept them, who created the earth, our home.

WHAT IS 'REVELATION'?

Revelation occurs when God becomes present to someone. It can happen at any time and any place, but it often happens in a time of crisis when we seem to be most open to God. We can only describe it as a moment in which we become aware of the presence of another person, a higher being. We know ourselves to be in the presence of a holy Other.

Out of this encounter with God a promise is born. We receive some message that relates very directly to our deepest concerns and needs. It was out of such an encounter that Abraham and Sarah received the promise.

But revelation is also related to our openness to God. If we are not open, the promises of God will not be met with faith, trust, and commitment. They will have no way of being fulfilled. Knowledge through revelation occurs only where there is revelation and an appropriate response of faith and trust to the revelation. But how does this work?

ESTABLISHING THE TRUTH OF REVELATION

Experiencing the presence of God and receiving the promise of God are subjective experiences. They can't be proved. What is required is an appropriate *response*. We need to believe the promise strongly enough to place our lives on it. Once we do that, it has the possibility of becoming reality.

If and when the promise is fulfilled, we gain knowledge. We call it knowledge because it has been fulfilled in events in history. We now know something about the promise and the one who gave the promise. We now know that the promise of God is true and we know that God is faithful and true.

Let's say I come to a bridge with a heavily loaded truck. I fear that the bridge may not be strong enough to carry the weight. So I go underneath the bridge to inspect it. I judge that the bridge promises to carry the load. I do not yet know this but I believe it to be true. The point is, I have to believe it strongly enough to return to the truck and drive across. I have to place my life on it! But if I do, and once I am across the bridge, I know it is strong

> "If we are to understand, we need to believe, and the fact of understanding reinforces our belief. In this way, then, we progress as though up a spiral staircase: We keep going round, but at each turn we progress further…. [The people who wrote the Bible] told of events, but these events took on meaning because they believed."
>
> Etienne Charpentier, *How to Read the Old Testament*

enough. If I had not responded to the promise I would have never known whether the promise was true.

The truth of the promise is confirmed through its fulfillment. When Abraham and Sarah received God's protection, a son, and land, the promise was confirmed, and they learned something about the character of God.

WITNESS TO REVELATION

The experience of Abraham and Sarah in responding to the promises of God has been repeated over and over. Other ways God was revealed and promised life to the people of Israel include:

- delivering them from slavery in Egypt
- establishing a covenant with them at Sinai
- leading them into the Promised Land
- giving them a king
- repeatedly sending prophets with a message from God

Through the fulfillment of these promises the people came to know that God was interested in their welfare. This was life-saving news! It was so important that it had to be shared with others.

As the truth of God's promises continued to be confirmed, a community of faith was born. The events of revelation became sacred to the community, who made sure those stories would not be forgotten by the next generations.

THE SCRIPTURES

At first the witness to the revelation was oral. People talked about it and shared it with others. Then they entrusted the transmission of the sacred stories to specific appointed persons, first priests and later scribes.

As time went on, certain parts of the sacred tradition were *written down*. Some of the laws and teachings were written down early. Songs and hymns used at public commemorations were also written down. These fragments of written material were later incorporated into the works of other writers.

Eventually, full-length documents were written. There were books of the law, of history, and of prophecy. There were also books we could call collections, such as the psalms, proverbs, and books of wisdom.

Finally there were so many writings that claimed to be from God that the people had to determine which ones were to be remembered. In this way the books that were regarded to be of God were established. The Jewish community accepted the Law, the Prophets, and the Writings as sacred books, as *canon*. Christians accepted the Jewish canon as well as the tradition about Jesus (the New Testament) as sacred books, as canon.

But just as God was not first revealed by a book, so is God not bound by the confines of written pages today. God is ever revealing love and promise, and is ever being revealed in the experiences of people of faith. Listen and look!

> "This marvelous anthology of books and letters called the Bible is all for the sake of astonishment! It's for divine transformation, not intellectual or 'small-self' coziness."
>
> Fr. Richard Rohr, OFM, *Things Hidden*

> God was not first revealed by a book, and is not confined by written pages. God is ever revealing love and promise. Listen and look!

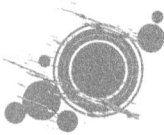

JOB RECOMMENDATION

You are an employer who's been asked to write a recommendation for the employee you just interviewed. Write your recommendation in the space below. Use the questions at the bottom to help you.

Name:

Position wanted:

Recommendation:

What did the employee say that most convinced you that s/he could do the job?

Did the employee make any promises? What were they? Why might you trust those promises?

Permission is granted to photocopy this handout for use with this session.

SESSION 2

WHAT MAKES A STORY HOLY? »»
The Bible as History

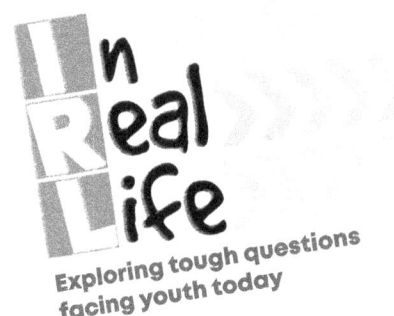
Exploring tough questions facing youth today

»» KEY VERSE

"The Lord your God will raise up for you from your own people a prophet like [Moses]. You must listen to whatever he tells you." (Acts 3:22)

»» FAITH STORY

Acts 3:11-26

»» FAITH FOCUS

The promises made by God to Abraham and Sarah as well as to Moses were still remembered in the time of the early church. They were the basis for understanding what God was doing in their own time. In Jesus' coming they saw the promises made to Moses, Abraham, and Sarah fulfilled. Knowing the stories and history of God's people, they could understand the working of God in the present.

»» SESSION GOAL

Help participants value biblical history as events handed down *from* a people of faith to *shape* a people of faith, and introduce them to Bible study resources.

»» BIBLE STUDY SKILLS to be practiced in this session: use of concordance, study Bible, and timeline of key events in the Bible.

»» Materials needed and advance preparation

- Copies of the handout sheet for Session 2
- Chalkboard/chalk or newsprint/markers
- Study Bibles, concordances
- Digital or phone camera (*Option A* in Respond)
- Index cards or slips of paper prepared with events/persons critical to Bible history (see Apply)

TEACHING PLAN

1. FOCUS 5 minutes

Pair up, and have each person interview the other about his/her family history. Note grandparents and great-grandparents. Then ask each one to share some incident or story that is meaningful to the family, a story they like to remember.

In Real Life | How to Read the Bible

> "By reading the Scriptures I am so renewed that all nature seems renewed around me and with me. The sky seems to be a pure, a cooler blue, the trees a deeper green. The whole world is charged with the glory of God and I feel fire and music under my feet."
>
> Thomas Merton

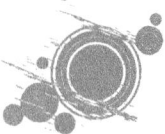

2. CONNECT 6-8 minutes

Share some of these stories with the group. Ask what is important about the story and why it was remembered whereas many other things were purposely forgotten or left out.

Shift to the next activity by saying: *The past is important to us, because it tells about who we are in the present. The people of God have been shaped by many events over a long period of time. The history of the people of God is remembered for generations to come. That's how the Bible came to be.*

3. EXPLORE THE BIBLE 10 minutes

The story of Pentecost was strange at best, but would have been just too weird to handle if the disciples had not known their history well enough to explain the context of the mysterious events.

First, help participants recall two New Testament stories: of Pentecost and of Peter's healing the blind beggar:

Pentecost
Just before Jesus ascended into heaven, he told the disciples to wait in Jerusalem until they would be baptized with the Holy Spirit (Acts 1:4). When the Spirit came upon the people, pandemonium broke out; people began to speak in other languages, and others did not know what to make of it. Some thought they were drunk! But Peter knew the scriptures and was reminded that the prophet Joel had spoken of just such an event happening in the future. Peter was able to help the people understand what God was doing because he knew the scriptures, the story of God's people.

Peter heals a crippled beggar
Another time, Peter healed a crippled beggar at the temple gate. People were amazed at what Peter had done and gathered about him. But Peter linked what he was doing to the history of God's people from the time of Abraham to the present. He said, "Why do you stare at us, as though by our own power or piety we had made him walk?" The power came from Jesus and not from themselves.

Peter then explained how the very God of Abraham, Isaac, and Jacob raised up Jesus from the dead and so fulfilled the word of the prophets when they spoke about the suffering servant of God. The events of Pentecost and the events of power (miracles) in the lives of the disciples could only be understood when seen as the fulfillment of God's promises spoken through the prophets.

Second, read through Acts 3:11-26 as a group.

Third, explain how Jesus was seen as the new Moses:

The people of the early church understood Jesus to be the promised messiah and son of David. He was seen as the king who was to come, the prince of peace (Isaiah 9:6), and the suffering servant (Isaiah 53).

But this Jesus was also the new Moses. He fulfilled the announcement made by Moses that there would come another prophet like himself who would speak for God (Deuteronomy 18:18). This is what Peter reminded the people of as they gathered about him.

Peter brought up the ancient covenant relationship between God and the people, the covenant established in the time of Moses. Everyone knew who Moses was, and how important the covenant was. Therefore, Peter was reminding the people of one of the most critical points in their history, in order to explain another critical point: the meaning of Jesus.

4. APPLY 10 minutes

This activity is intended to help participants learn to use a concordance to recall the chronology of important biblical events and persons, and to see how history helps define contemporary life.

Write down on index cards or slips of paper what you as leader take to be the high points of Israel's history. (A possible list: patriarchs, the exodus, Sinai, the entrance into the promised land, the time of Saul, David and Solomon, the division of the kingdom, the fall of the Northern Kingdom, the exile of the Southern Kingdom, the liberation under Cyrus, the reign of the Seleucid emperors, the reign of the Roman legates and procurators, the coming of Jesus, Paul's ministry, the growth of the early church.) Prepare enough cards to supply one to each person in the group. If you have a very small group, consider giving each person more than one card.

Give each person one card, a copy of the handout sheet for Session 2, a study Bible, and a concordance. Explain that they can look up a word or subject in the concordance (which is arranged in alphabetical order), and find a list of the Bible passages where that word occurs. Using the concordance, they are to find Bible passages that relate to the event or person(s) on their card. They are to find and study the passage(s) and come up with a symbol (something found in the meeting room or something they draw themselves) of their event/person.

Extra challenge option #1: Add into the mix of cards, books and events from the intertestamental period. Make sure you have Bibles with the Deuterocanonical books.

Extra challenge option #2: Search scriptural allusions indexes in song books to find familiar songs that allude to the events/persons listed on the cards.

5. RESPOND 10 minutes

>> **Option A:** Have the group work together to make a **human timeline** using their event/person cards and symbols. They could also add dates where possible, but it is more important to get the order of events right. If your group is very small and you had them study more than one event/person card, have them do the exercise a couple of times, using different cards for each new timeline. You might take a picture of the timeline, using a digital or phone camera, and have a poster-sized print made to put on your meeting room wall for a ready-made timeline to which you can refer throughout the study.

>> **Option B:** (for youth meeting/retreat):

Make a video for younger children in your church that tells of some of the "high points" of biblical history. Show participants holding up their symbols, retelling their stories, and putting themselves into a human timeline. In this way, older youth in the church are passing on important Bible stories to younger children in the church, and doing so in a way that shows the value of remembering history.

Suggested benediction: *God blesses us by giving us memory. Remember and tell others the stories of God and God's people.*

INSIGHTS FROM SCRIPTURE

What stories did the people consider important enough to retain for future generations?

›› THE STORY OF THE PATRIARCHS

The story of the patriarchs (Genesis 12–50) are key to understanding the Hebrew Bible. These are background stories we need to know in order to understand the ancient testimony, just as the Hebrew Bible itself contains the stories necessary for us to understand Jesus and the coming of the Holy Spirit.

›› THE REVELATION OF GOD THROUGH THE EXODUS

The action of God to save and to redeem a slave people made a lasting impression. Through this event they knew that God was not linked with the rich and the powerful, but had compassion on the poor and the powerless. Through this event they knew that God comes to save those who are lost and unable to save themselves.

›› THE REVELATION OF GOD AT SINAI

This was the establishment of the ancient covenant. God promised to be there for the people of Israel in times of need, to hear them whenever they called for help. In addition, God gave the gracious gift of the law, explaining what behaviors would lead to life and what acts would lead to death. In return, the people responded by promising to be God's people, and to keep all that the Lord had commanded.

›› LOOK AHEAD

For the next session's Connect activity, *Option A*, you'll need a newspaper or news magazine, showing a variety of news reporting forms (editorial, obituary, ads, features, etc.).

›› THE ENTRANCE INTO THE LAND

The books of Joshua and Judges tell about the entrance into the Promised Land, and the four books of Samuel and Kings tell the story of the kings in Israel, including the great kings David and Solomon. The books are full of stories of temptation, falling away from God, and returning to the covenant. In short, it is a history of the human struggle to be faithful.

›› THE WORD OF GOD THROUGH THE PROPHETS

Responding to the failure of the kings to maintain the covenant, God sent prophets to remind people of what behavior is life-affirming and which is life-denying. The messages of the prophets were not only calls to conversion, but also promises of sustenance when the people of God were scattered by the exile. They thus became a very important part of the sacred tradition in Israel.

›› THE WORD OF THE WISE

Israel remembered the past and expressed faith and community life through worship. Their hymns, or psalms, expressed both praise and lament. David was credited with collecting many of these psalms. There were also people who were keen observers of life. They made common sense observations of what actions would lead to blessing and what actions would separate people from their Creator. Solomon collected many of these wise sayings, or proverbs.

There were other writings grouped as wisdom literature. All of these writings were included in what the Jewish people knew as the TaNaK, a word that stood for the Law, the Prophets, and the Writings.

OTHER STORIES OF FAITH

After the exile, the Seleucid emperors tried to eliminate the Jewish faith by force. There seemed to be no hope for the people. But the people knew God was faithful and they believed that the promises of God would somehow be fulfilled in some cataclysmic action in the future.

This gave rise to three different responses. There were the Maccabees who resorted to revolt, rebellion, and armed conflict; others, like the writer of the book of Daniel, believed that one should simply remain faithful to God under a heathen people, and God would restore Israel. Another group emphasizing purity and self-denial withdrew to Qumran to practice a life of ritual purity.

All of them, however, took comfort in an *apocalyptic* view of the future. They believed that God would wipe out evil on the earth and then the promises of God given by the prophets would be fulfilled.

Some of the literature that emerged during this period of trouble and suffering include historical accounts of the Maccabees (First and Second Maccabees), legendary or novelistic writings (Judith and Tobit), and wisdom sayings (Sirach, Wisdom of Solomon). These six books and the book of the prophet Baruch are considered *deuterocanonical* by Catholics. In Protestant Bibles, they are often found under the heading "Apocrypha."

There are other religious writings from this period such as the books of Enoch that are not considered canonical, but provide us with valuable information about the history and religious imagination of the people of this time. Many of these can be found among the books contained in the Dead Sea Scrolls.

During the time of Jesus and the early church, something similar happened. There were not only the writings that we now have in the New Testament but many others who wrote gospels (e.g. Gospel of Thomas, Gospel of Mary Magdalene), epistles, and acts. But these additional writings were judged by the later church not to be authoritative and were excluded from the canon. We have these writings today in the Apocrypha.

Parts of the Bible

- **Books of Moses or The Law (Pentateuch):** Genesis, Exodus, Leviticus, Numbers, Deuteronomy
- **Books of History:** Joshua, Judges, Ruth, 1 & 2 Samuel, 1 & 2 Kings, 1 & 2 Chronicles, Ezra, Nehemiah, Tobit, Judith, Esther, 1&2 Maccabees
- **Books of Poetry and Wisdom:** Job, Psalms, Proverbs, Ecclesiastes, Song of Solomon, Wisdom of Solomon, Sirach, Lamentations
- **Books of Prophecy:** (There are 18, beginning with Isaiah, ending with Malachi)
- **Gospels:** Matthew, Mark, Luke, John
- **Acts:** (of the Apostles, story of early Christian church)
- **Letters:** (also called epistles. There are 22, beginning with Romans, ending with Revelation.)

> "It was a non-Christian, Mahatma Gandhi, who once said: 'You Christians look after a document containing enough dynamite to blow all civilization to pieces, turn the world upside down, and bring peace to a battle-torn planet. But you treat it as though it is nothing more than a piece of literature.'"

Pope Francis,
Introduction to the YouCat Bible

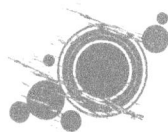

Sharpening Your Study Skills

Exploring tough questions facing youth today

Bible study resources can help you make sense of the events of biblical history, as well as give clues as to why the stories of the Bible have meaning today.

Bible study help	What's it for?
Study Bible	Gives context of stories and events with maps, footnotes, and charts.
Concordance	Lists words found in the Bible followed by all the verses in the Bible where that word is used. Arranged alphabetically.
Bible dictionary	Gives definitions of words found in the Bible.
Bible commentary	Explanations of Bible passages. There are one-volume commentaries, as well as more detailed commentaries devoted to just one book of the Bible.
Parallel Bible	Sets different versions/translations of the Bible side by side, so you can compare.
Bible companion or handbook	Contains cultural notes, maps, and charts.

Parts of the Bible

- **Books of Moses or The Law (Pentateuch):** Genesis, Exodus, Leviticus, Numbers, Deuteronomy
- **Books of History:** Joshua, Judges, Ruth, 1 & 2 Samuel, 1 & 2 Kings, 1 & 2 Chronicles, Ezra, Nehemiah, Tobit, Judith, Esther, 1&2 Maccabees
- **Books of Poetry and Wisdom:** Job, Psalms, Proverbs, Ecclesiastes, Song of Solomon, Wisdom of Solomon, Sirach
- **Books of Prophecy:** (There are 18, beginning with Isaiah, ending with Malachi)
- **Gospels:** Matthew, Mark, Luke, John
- **Acts:** (of the Apostles, story of early Christian church)
- **Letters:** (also called epistles. There are 22, beginning with Romans, ending with Revelation.)

Permission is granted to photocopy this handout for use with this session.

>>> **SESSION 3**

HOW DO YOU HEAR? >>>

The Bible as Literature

>>> KEY VERSES

All scripture is inspired by God and is useful for teaching, for reproof, for correction, and for training in righteousness, so that everyone who belongs to God may be proficient, equipped for every good work. (2 Timothy 3:16-17)

>>> FAITH STORY

Micah 6:1-8; 2 Timothy 3:10-17; Psalm 119:105

>>> FAITH FOCUS

Paul did not hesitate to refer to his life as exemplary for other Christians. He knew the scriptures, first as a trained Pharisee, and then as a follower of Jesus Christ. He knew that the Bible spoke in many different ways to many different situations in life. The biblical writers wanted to make sure that their message about God was heard and understood, so they chose different literary forms for different messages. Those forms would tell the reader how to interpret the message.

>>> SESSION GOAL

Introduce participants to the various genre and forms of literature used in the Bible and how the form indicates how the message is to be understood.

>>> BIBLE STUDY SKILLS to be practiced in this session: recognition of different types of Bible literature (genre), use of commentaries.

>>> Materials needed and advance preparation

- Copies of the handout sheet for Session 3
- One egg
- Stopwatch or watch with second hand
- News or magazine stories (*Option A* in Connect)
- Bibles
- Variety of one-volume Bible commentaries (or other commentaries)
- Writing paper, pencils
- Chalkboard/chalk or newsprint/marker

TEACHING PLAN

1. FOCUS 3-5 minutes

Divide into two teams for a sort of one-round "Scattergories" game. Give paper and a pencil to one person on each team.

Hold up an egg and a stopwatch or watch with a second hand. Tell the group that each team must list as many different ways of serving the egg as they can think of. Allow 30 seconds.

Call time, and have one team name their culinary delights, and list them on chalkboard or newsprint. Then have the other team list their dishes. Whenever there is a duplicate, put a check mark beside the first list, and do not list that egg dish again. When both teams have given their lists, circle the unique dishes given by each team, and award a point for each. Team with the most points wins.

Point out how the egg, though still an egg, can be served up in many different forms. Some people appreciate some ways of serving the egg better than others.

> "To search out the intention of the sacred writers, attention should be given, among other things, to 'literary forms.' For truth is set forth and expressed differently in texts which are variously historical, prophetic, poetic, or of other forms of discourse."
>
> *Dogmatic Constitution on Divine Revelation,* 12.

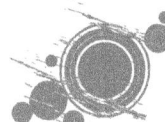

2. CONNECT 5-10 minutes

>> **Option A:** Ask the group to list as many forms of **news reporting** they can think of in 30 seconds (may include headline news, obituaries, editorials, ads, features, etc.). Write them on the chalkboard or newsprint as people call them out. Then go on to *"For All Options,"* below.

>> **Option B:** Ask the group to list as many types of **social media** they can think of in 30 seconds (might include Facebook, Twitter, Tumblr, Snapchat, etc.). Write them on the chalkboard or newsprint as people call them out. Then go on to *"For All Options,"* below.

>> **Option C:** Ask the group to list as many types of **TV** they can think of in 30 seconds (might include sitcom, drama, action, anime, news, documentaries, etc.). Write them on the chalkboard or newsprint as people call them out. Then go on to *"For All Options,"* below.

>> **Option D:** Ask the group to list as many types of **music** they can think of in 30 seconds (might include hip-hop, folk, disco, jazz, opera, country, blues, rock, dubstep, etc.). Write them on the chalkboard or newsprint as people call them out. Then go on to *"For All Options,"* below.

>> **For All Options:** Point out that news reporting, social media, TV, and music all give us excellent practice in recognizing different forms of communication. Depending on the media form (social media, TV, music) you focused on, ask group members to name their favorite type. Ask, *Why do you like it? What about it grabs your attention? What about it speaks to you? What type do you feel you understand best?* Get the group talking about the merits of different forms of communication (or genre).

Shift to the next activity by saying: *An egg, a story, and music can all be served up in different ways, and can give different messages. It's the same with the Bible.*

3. EXPLORE THE BIBLE 25 minutes

Point out that just like media today, the Bible uses different *forms* to send the message. If we recognize the form, we're more likely to understand what was intended by the writer. For example, if someone tried to tell you an ad or commercial was hard news, you'd be skeptical. If someone told you a prophecy in the form of a funeral dirge, you'd know right away that it wasn't good news. The Bible has all kinds of ways of presenting its message: predictions, hymns, obituaries, love songs, short stories with a moral, myths, court transcripts, and battle accounts, just to name a few.

Distribute writing paper and have participants fold the paper into thirds lengthwise, so they have three columns, labeled A, B, and C. Next, distribute copies of the handout sheet and assign each person one or two scriptures from the list provided on pages 19-20. Have Bible commentaries available. (One-volume commentaries may be easiest to collect.)

Instruct participants to study each Bible passage following the directions on the handout sheet. They will:

1. Write in **Column A** what form of communication, or *genre*, they believe is represented by that passage

   (Example: Micah 6:1-8 looks like a poem, but is a lawsuit/court case [see below])

2. Look up the passage in a commentary to get a second opinion, and write that form in **Column B**

3. (**Column C** will be filled in during Apply.)

Walk them through the process with this example from Micah 6:1-8:

> [God] has told you, O mortal, what is good;
> and what does the Lord require of you but to do justice, and to love kindness, and to walk humbly with your God? (Micah 6:8)

Ask if they can recognize the form of the literature. They probably will not be able to do so. Then explain in your own words: *These words are the conclusion of a court case that God brings against the people of Israel. The people would have recognized by the form of the literature that God was taking them to court and that they had to answer the charge against them.*

To bring home the action of the passage, act out the elements of this lawsuit, according to the chart below. Have someone read the parts of the prosecutor (God), bailiff, defendant, and judge, as though they were in a courtroom. Explain how God took the people to court because they had let their spiritual and community responsibilities slide. God, who had given them no reason to turn to other gods, wanted the whole cosmos to know that they were unjust in turning away. God brought a few proofs to bear (including their liberation from Egypt), and then the people answered the charges. In the end, all God asked for was integrity in the covenant relationship: justice, mercy, and proper humility before God.

The prophet's use of a lawsuit (Micah 6:1-8)

The call to hear (*Bailiff*)	Hear what the Lord says:
Summons to trial (*Bailiff to prosecutor*)	Rise, plead your case before the mountains and let the hills hear your voice.
To witnesses/jury (*Bailiff*)	Hear, you mountains, the controversy of the Lord, and you enduring foundations of the earth;
Reason	for the Lord has a controversy with his people, and he will contend with Israel.
God's charge (*Prosecutor*)	(the charge is assumed to be that the people deserted God)
Thus God's Question (*Prosecutor*)	O my people, what have I done to you? In what have I wearied you? Answer me!
Testimony Proper (*Prosecutor*)	For I brought you up out of the land of Egypt, and redeemed you from the house of slavery; (etc. through verse 5)
The People inquire of God (*Defendant*)	With what shall I come before the Lord, and bow myself before God on high? (etc. through verse 7)
God answers (*Judge or Prosecutor*)	He has told you, O mortal, what is good; and what does the Lord require of you but to do justice, and to love kindness, and to walk humbly with your God?

Keep your concordances on hand for the next session, and make two posters labeled "right" and "wrong," respectively.

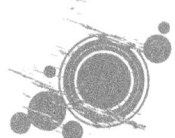

Use these Bible passages (and/or others you choose) to highlight different forms (or genres) of Bible literature:

- *Narrative/saga*: Genesis 2:4b-25; Joshua 2:1-24; Exodus 7:1-13, 12:33-42, 14; Luke 9:10-17; Matthew 3:13-17
- *Genealogy*: Genesis 10:1-5
- *Short story*: Genesis 11:1-9
- *Parable*: Judges 9:7-15; Ezekiel 37:1-14; Matthew 21:28-32; Luke 8:4-8
- *Covenant, or apodictic law*: Exodus 20:1-17
- *Wisdom literature*: Proverbs 13:1-5
- *Love song*: Song of Solomon 7:10-13, 8:6-7, 5:10-16
- *Hymn*: Luke 1:46-55 (Magnificat); Philippians 2:6-11 (Christ hymn); Exodus 15:21; Psalm 23, 135; John 12:12-15
- *Prophecy*: Jeremiah 31:31-34; Revelation 1:9-20; Luke 7:27; Acts 15:16-18
- *Miracle story*: Daniel 3:23-27; Luke 6:6-10; John 6:1-14
- *Kerygma, or preaching*: Acts 4:8-12; Colossians 3:5-11
- *Obituary*: Deuteronomy 34:5-12
- *Letter/epistle*: 1 Corinthians 1:2-3, 16:19-21; Philippians 1:1-2, 4:21-23
- *Poetry*: Isaiah 49:8-9; Exodus 15:1-5; Ecclesiastes 3:1-8; Matthew 6:9-13
- *Legal instruction*: Leviticus13:47-59; Deuteronomy 22:8-12, Deuteronomy 5:6-21; Exodus 20:1-17
- *Acts*: Acts 19:1-7

4. APPLY 5 minutes

After they have decided what genre they are dealing with, have them come up with a contemporary parallel genre, and list in it **Column C**. They can either think of one themselves, or find a parallel in the news media examples. For example, the Micah 6:1-8 passage above is poetry that is also a lawsuit. A contemporary parallel could be the opening arguments by the prosecution in a court case. Another example: Proverbs 12:17-18 are two pithy sayings that reflect everyday, practical experience or inspiration. They could compare to a message on posters.

Option: Bring in a portable radio, and channel surf until the group finds a station that is broadcasting something that parallels the genre of their assigned Bible passage (news, music, announcements, commentary, etc.). List what you found in Column C.

5. RESPOND 5 minutes

Have each person *read* part or all of their assigned passage (depending on the length and the number of people in your group) according to its type of genre. For example, if they have an obituary, they should read slowly and solemnly. If it is a love song, they should read passionately. If it is a battle account, they might read it like a news reporter. But if it is a battle account that is also an epic, it should be read like a cheerleader trying to whip up support for the hero.

Close with a prayer thanking God for speaking in the Bible in many ways, and for giving us tools with which to study God's word. "Your word is a lamp to my feet, and a light to my path" (Psalm 119:105).

Suggested benediction: *In the Bible, God has many methods of getting through to us. Those who have ears, hear.*

 INSIGHTS FROM SCRIPTURE

The message of scripture is always encased in a form (genre) appropriate to the message. This form indicates how the message is to be understood.

GENRE OF THE HEBREW BIBLE

NARRATIVES

Close to half of the Hebrew Bible consists of narratives of various kinds. The historical narratives deal with events and people in the life of Israel and the early church. Telling stories about the past helps reveal God's plan and purpose. For example, the exodus narrative underlines God's action to liberate a slave people. The exile, on the other hand, underlines an experience of God's judgment. Some narratives will fall under the category of an *epic*. An epic relates the past, but its motive is to rouse enthusiasm and highlight heroes, and may even exaggerate the story to achieve that aim.

LAW

God's will for the people was expressed in the law of the covenant. It was stated in two basic forms—casuistic and apodictic. The *casuistic* law was stated in an "If...then" form. If you had done thus or so, the consequence would be such and such. Most of the laws are given in this form.

The *apodictic* laws were stated in an absolute form. The Ten Commandments are examples. They state an absolute command—"You shall not kill"—and in that way express the intention of God for all people at all times.

God gave the law in order to show what actions would lead to life and what actions would lead in the direction of death. God invited us to choose life. That means choosing the restrictions of the law so as to promote life as God intended it.

POETRY

Poetry has its own subset of different forms. There are prayers, songs, dirges, and liturgies that use poetry. Poetry uses uniformity of length of line, rhythm, and meter to express deep emotion and thought.

Much of the poetry of the Hebrew Bible is in the form of parallelism. It is given in two or more lines in which the second line is used to restate, augment, or extend the thought of the first line. Thus Psalm 24:3 asks:

> *Who shall ascend the hill of the Lord?*
> *And who shall stand in his holy place?*

The second line is synonymous with the first. Another type of parallel contrasts two ideas, as in Proverbs 20:29:

> *The glory of youth is their strength,*
> *but the beauty of the aged is their gray hair.*

The thought can also be balanced, extended, or interpreted in the second line. Always it contains the clue as to how to read the verse.

» PROPHECY

In the genre of prophecy, many different forms are also used. Micah resorts to the use of a prophetic lawsuit (Micah 6:1-8). Amos conducts a prophetic disputation (Amos 3:1-5) and Jeremiah gives us a prophetic liturgy, or order of worship.

The prophets did not only predict future events. They were mainly concerned with pointing out how and where the people were transgressing the covenant with God. They warned the people about judgment if they did not correct their ways. We need to read their writings as interpreting for us the meaning of the covenant relationship with God.

» WISDOM

The books of Psalms, Proverbs, Ecclesiastes, Lamentations, Job, etc., belong to the wisdom genre of literature. They are observations about life. Thus in Proverbs there are truths that come from years of experience. They can be compared to the scientific method in that we observe, formulate, and state as fact those things that we have been able to confirm. Notice that wisdom in the biblical sense is particularly concerned with people and relationships, and comes to pithy conclusions like social or behavioral scientists might.

GENRE OF THE NEW TESTAMENT

» GOSPELS

It seems as if the Gospel writers had to choose a specific form of writing to be able to encase the work of Jesus in his ministry. The four Gospels each tell the story of Jesus, but each one tells it differently and for a different purpose. They each present a window through which we can observe the life of Jesus.

Jesus spoke in parables, stories to help people think of God and the reign of God in an entirely different way. The best way was to tell stories in such a way that people could envision life in relation to God other than in legal terms. Jesus invited people to relate to God personally, directly, and wholeheartedly the way he did.

» ACTS

Acts calls attention to the work of the Holy Spirit in the church and in the world. It shows how the church grew through the work of the Holy Spirit in the church. Acts is literature that points beyond the events to the principal agent of the church, the Holy Spirit. The New Testament Apocrypha has other "Acts" books.

» EPISTLES (OR LETTERS)

Once early church communities were established, Paul and the apostles continued to nurture them through their visits and their writing of letters, called epistles. Writers used the letter styles of that day, like a variety of today's social media that "gets the word out" and can connect people who are otherwise scattered geographically.

The epistles are based on the tradition about Jesus which the apostles communicated to the church in the founding of the church (1 Corinthians 15:3-5). They are further instructions and advice given by the writers and help us know how to interpret the Gospels.

REVELATION

Revelation belongs to apocalyptic literature. As such it resorts to dualistic language, to animal imagery, symbolic presentation, and as dreams and visions. Its main purpose, however, is prophetic, as Revelation 1:3 indicates. It interprets what is of God and what is not of God in the churches; it encourages the people to be faithful to God. It encourages them in the face of persecution and proclaims that the victory of Christ over the powers of evil has already been won in Christ's death on the cross (5:1-14).

Genre and Forms of Literature in the Bible

In Real Life
Exploring tough questions facing youth today

HEBREW BIBLE

GENRE	FORMS
Narratives	Reports
	Heroic narrative
	Prophetic narratives
Law	Casuistic laws
	Apodictic laws
	Legal instruction
Poetry	Prayers
	Songs/psalms
	Liturgies, etc.
Prophecy	Woe speeches
	Funeral dirge
	Prophetic disputation
	Prophetic lawsuit
Wisdom	Proverbs
	Parallelism

NEW COVENANT

GENRE	FORMS
Gospels	Miracles
	Parables
	Birth accounts
Acts	Narrative
	Sermons
	Testimonies
Epistles (Letters)	Hymns
	Creeds
	Kerygma (Preaching or sermons)
Revelation	Visions/dreams
	Woes
	Letters

These are only some of the forms used. Can you name other genre or forms?

Tips for studying Bible passages:

- Simply read, paying no attention to anything in the margins or footnotes. Ask yourself: What is the passage talking about? What do you like about it? What amazes you? Who are the characters? What are they doing? What is happening? Write down questions you have.

   A. Write in **Column A** what form of communication, or genre, you believe is represented by that passage.

   B. Look up the passage in a commentary to get a second opinion, and write that form in **Column B**. Recheck the passage to find out what kind of truth it is trying to convey.

   C. (**Column C** will be filled in later.)

Permission is granted to photocopy this handout for use with this session.

>>> **SESSION 4**

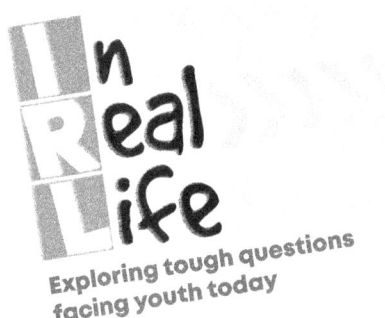

WHAT'S IN IT FOR ME? >>>

The Bible as Foundation for Living

>>> **KEY VERSES**

As he who called you is holy, be holy yourselves in all your conduct; for it is written, "You shall be holy, for I am holy." (1 Peter 1:15-16)

>>> **FAITH STORY**

1 Peter 1:13-16; Colossians 3:1-17

>>> **FAITH FOCUS**

Peter and Paul have given us a way of thinking about right and wrong, good and evil. They start from the premise that humans were created in the image of God, and created to be morally responsible persons in accordance with the righteousness of God. The Bible reveals to us the character of God shown in God's acts and as embodied in Jesus, and then indicates that we are to become God-like and Christ-like in character. That is what Peter told the early Christians, but he used a passage that goes all the way back to the law of Moses.

>>> **SESSION GOAL**

Develop in participants an understanding for ethics, and show that the character of God (as revealed in the Bible) is the basis for our own character and action.

>>> **BIBLE STUDY SKILLS** to be practiced in this session: use of concordance to make a list of characteristics of the holy life.

>>> **Materials needed and advance preparation**

- Copies of the handout sheet for Session 4
- Two large sheets of paper and markers
- Bible concordances
- Bibles
- Two boxes of dress-up clothes, scarves, pieces of fabric
- Two privacy screens (*Option B* in Explore)
- Writing paper, pencils

TEACHING PLAN

1. FOCUS 5 minutes

Post two large sheets of paper marked "right" and "wrong" respectively, and distribute markers. Ask everyone to write normative statements on the respective sheets about what they hold to be right or wrong. For example: "Killing a person is wrong" or "Telling the truth is right."

2. CONNECT 5-7 minutes

Once everyone has written their statements, go back over each one and ask whether they agree with the statements written. Many of the statements made will no doubt be disputed. Where there are differences, ask how they would resolve the differences. To what would they appeal? Tradition? The laws of the land? The church? The Bible?

If the suggestion is made that ethics comes from the Bible, ask: *How do we know what the Bible teaches about ethics?* It will immediately be clear that the Bible does not speak directly to most of the questions of ethics that we raise or that are on the sheets of paper.

Shift to the next activity by saying: *We often look for a set of "do's" and "don'ts" by which to live, but it would be impossible for such a list to cover everything in a fast-changing world. The Bible, which is a guide for faith and practice, approaches ethics from a different angle.*

3. EXPLORE THE BIBLE 20-25 minutes.

Option A: Offer the following mini-lecture:

Peter's approach to ethics (*or holiness*) in 1 Peter 1:13-16

Peter begins his letter by affirming that people have all come to newness of life through the resurrection of Jesus from the dead (1:3). This is the gift of God to us. This is what the prophets talked about but which they could not yet fully understand (1 Peter 1:10-12). This new life in Christ means that we live by a different ethic. As new persons in Christ, we have received a new nature and are now different in character than we were before. What is that new character like? We are to be holy as God is holy (1 Peter 1:16). How does that happen? Peter says that in order to be holy we don't have to *get more holiness* (1 Peter 2:11-12; 4:3). Instead, we need to *get rid of* (put off) those things that come from the character we once were and let the new character in Christ shine forth.

Paul's call to holiness (*or ethical living*) in Colossians 3:1-17

For Paul, holiness (or being ethical) was a question of being related to Christ. If you were raised to newness of life in Christ you would seek the things that are of God. The one who is in Christ is informed and formed by Christ's character.

Purification, or sanctification, consists of two actions, according to Paul. There are those things that we are to "put off" (Colossians 3:5-11) and those things that we are to "put on" (Colossians 3:12-17). The people of God were to cleanse themselves from the evil characteristics of their former life.

Continue with *Option A* in Apply.

Option B: Put on a **fashion show**, Colossians-style. Colossians 3:5-17 consists of two lists: one outlines behavior *inappropriate* for Christians, and the other lists behaviors we are to "put on," or how we are to behave as Christians.

Break into two groups of "models," and hand each group a box of clothes, a Bible, a piece of paper, and a pencil. Set up the privacy screens for models to "change clothes," or go behind a door or couch. A large group can provide its own human privacy screen.

Group One will search **Colossians 3:5-11**, and name up to four behaviors that Christians are called to "put off." List behaviors on a piece of paper.

For each behavior, come up with an "outfit" to represent that behavior, and pick a person to model it.

MORAL DEVELOPMENT IN TEENS

Recent research links types of video games teens played, how long they played them, and teens' levels of moral reasoning: their ability to take the perspective of others into account. Violent video games delay development of moral judgment in teens.

The research, published in Educational Media International, recommends that teachers, parents, and teens work together to provide the different social opportunities players seem to be lacking. Charity work, community involvement, and extracurricular activities all provide gamers with "different perspectives and positive role-taking opportunities."

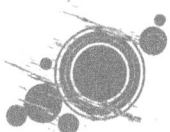

Group Two's passage is **Colossians 3:12-17**. Name ways of being that new people in Christ are to "put on." They could add the qualities observed in the beatitudes (Matthew 5:1-12) or the qualities mentioned as fruits of the Spirit (Galatians 5:22-23).

Have each group choose an emcee, or announcer, to talk their models down the runway, explaining their outfits. The models should ham it up, as they model "clothing" from their box in a way that symbolizes the behavior from the Colossians passages. Alternate groups so that the group modeling "put off" behaviors contrasts with the group modeling "put on" behaviors. Keep the number of models to a maximum of eight, or have two models walking the runway at the same time, modeling two different interpretations of the same behavior.

Conclude the show, and have everyone put clothes back in boxes and return to their groups. Finish by making the point that we can neither put on nor take off behaviors by our own strength. It comes through forgiveness (3:13), through clothing yourself in love (3:14), and through letting the peace of God rule in our hearts (3:15). We are in a sense to let God cleanse us from the things that lead to death (are unclean) and create a new spirit in us that is conformed to Christ. That is why we are to let the word of God dwell in us richly (3:16).

Once we let God purify us and our whole character, then we will be thankful and we will sing spiritual songs to God (3:16). When our ethic has become part and parcel of our character, who we are in Christ will be seen in all of our actions and in all of our speech (3:17).

Continue with *Option B* in Apply.

4. APPLY 7-10 minutes

Option A: Involve participants in a magazine or Internet search for clothing ads, and have them mention a few that attract them particularly and explain why. Then ask, *What choices do these ads want you to make and why?* Invite participants to assess critically what values the ads are asking them to "model." Then have them do cursory Internet research about where and how that clothing is manufactured. They could even look at clothing labels on what they are wearing at the moment. For example, what are the indications the clothing is or is not produced in a sweatshop that exploits female or child workers in another country? Does the company focus on quality and sustainable fibers or materials in its product? Get participants thinking about how their clothing choices align with "putting on" clothing that reflects the character of God.

Continue with *For Both Options*, below.

Option B: Have everyone stay in their "modeling" groups and see that each group has access to a concordance. Have them look up the word **become** to locate still more passages that tell us how we are to "put on" the character of God. Have them add to the lists of behaviors generated in the Explore activities. For example, Paul advises Christians to clothe themselves with compassion, kindness, humility, meekness, and patience. These *ways of being* outlined in the Bible guided many Christians in the past, especially when they were in crisis. It's one thing to make a list of ways to be, but it takes planning and practice to follow through.

Continue with *For Both Options*, below.

For Both Options: The Bible is about God, and how God wants us to live. Therefore, learning to read the Bible means learning to cue in to passages that give us direction for our lives. The Bible doesn't tell us so much what to do along every step of the way as it does give us an idea of how to *be* in a given situation.

These *ways of being* outlined in the Bible guided many Christians in the past. Christians who suffered for their faith, who sat in jails or faced torture for their beliefs, had to decide *before*

> "Read with attention! Do not stay on the surface as if reading a comic book! Never just skim the Word of God! Ask yourself: 'What does this say to my heart? Does God speak through these words to me? Has he touched me in the depths of my longing? What should I do?' Only in this way can the force of the Word of God unfold. Only in this way can it change our lives, making them great and beautiful."
>
> Pope Francis
> *Introduction to the YouCat Bible*

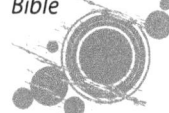

they were put to the test how they hoped they would behave under pressure. For example, when Martin Luther King Jr., was in jail, he planned ways for how he would nonviolently confront violence.

Have participants name one or two situations (confronting violence at school or at home, how to respond when offered drugs or alcohol, etc.) for which they need preparation in how to respond, how to *be* in that situation. Have them refer to their "modeling" lists and make a four-step plan for dealing with the situation they chose.

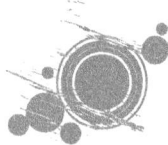

> "The glory of God is a human being fully alive."
>
> St. Ireneus

5. RESPOND 5 minutes

Compose a litany or worship chant (even a rap or cheer) that includes the phrases from the Bible that clue us in on how to be like the character of God in Jesus. Close with your litany.

Suggested benediction: *God has told you what is good. Put on the character of God, and live as God's child.*

INSIGHTS FROM SCRIPTURE

The story of creation affirms that God created all manner of life as well as ecosystems to support life on earth. God was clearly interested in life in all its fullness. The world and all that God has made is an expression of God's character.

In creating the world God has also created the moral order, and human beings as moral agents. As such, humans could choose to do good or evil, to say yes or no to God. Every day we make choices that reflect our character and our values. God honors us as persons and honors the choices we make. Nevertheless, if we choose what is life-denying instead of what is life-affirming, we face the consequences. But no matter what, God's intention continues to be fullness of life for us—even if we reject it.

LOOK AHEAD

Gather a variety of Bible translations for comparison during the next session.

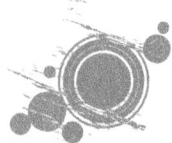

» LETTER OF THE LAW OR THE SPIRIT?

Leviticus 13:44 stands in the midst of laws that describe what is clean and what is unclean—foods and animals (Lev. 11), purification of women after childbirth (12), and disease (13). The detailed list of laws was a daily visual and physical reminder that God is a holy God.

The language and practice remained alive until the time of Christ. When the scribes and Pharisees criticized Jesus about the way he did and did not keep the law, he reminded them that God does not want people to put on a performance without any heart in it.

The Bible passages for this session point us in the right direction. Rather than toe the line to a complex system of laws, being God's children is a way of *being*. Peter indicated that we are to be holy as God is holy. That means we are to become God-like and Christ-like in character. To study the Bible is to learn to know who God is in character. God's character, righteousness, love, and grace are revealed to us in the events of history. Then, once we know who God is, we can know what we are to be.

WHAT IS GOD'S CHARACTER?

Abraham learned that God is a God who *promises life* to the people. To put on the character of God means that we will make—and keep—promises of life to others. Such promises may include giving food to the hungry, clothing the naked, befriending the friendless, accepting the rejected, caring for creation.

God liberated the children of Israel from slavery in Egypt. Act on behalf of God to *set people free* from prisons of loneliness, fear, despair, hopelessness, emptiness, drugs, materialism, individualism.

God covenanted to be our God. God covenanted *to be there for us* at all times and to lead us towards life. Some of us have been taught to feel guilt and shame when we do things wrong, that God gets angry and disappointed with us. The Bible teaches that the character of the Creator is loving and forgiving, a God who loves us during our good days and our bad days, who doesn't know how to do anything but love. Promise people that you will always be there for their good; that you will seek to speak the truth to them in love; that you will walk with them in the way of peace and life. Be there for people even when they are marching in the direction of death. It takes courage to speak for God in such times. Dare to be God's spokesperson, calling the world back from its wars, walls, and want.

WHAT IS CHRIST'S CHARACTER?

Paul, on the basis of the revelation received in Christ, said that we are to be Christ-like in character. In Colossians 3 he listed the virtues of the Christian life. These virtues are not so much rules to follow as they are ways of *being*. From our Christ-like being are to flow words and deeds that are in harmony with the character of God.

In Jesus, God showed us a new way, a new life. In him we could see yet more clearly what we as humans were created by God to be. Now we are called to follow Jesus and to be his disciples. Model for others a new life. Be Christ-like so that others will see Christ in you.

Dare to be God's spokesperson calling the world back from its wars, walls, and want.

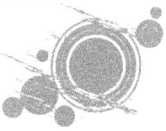

"I can learn to truly respect others. At times, I can simply be a sounding board for them, helping them to work through their problems peaceably. I can create art that brings attention to individuals who may not have found a voice for themselves. Through such efforts, I mirror the life of Jesus in my own unique way and at least make a corner of the world a bit more peaceful."

Gabriella Stocksdale, 15, Elgin, IL

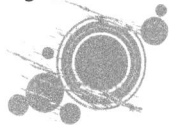

WHAT'S IN IT FOR ME?

The Bible as Foundation for Living

The Bible is about God, and how God wants us to live. Therefore, learning to read the Bible means learning to cue in to passages that give us direction for our lives. The Bible doesn't tell us so much what to do along every step of the way as it does give us an idea of how *to be* in a given situation.

Some of us have been taught to feel guilt and shame when we do things wrong, that God gets angry and disappointed with us. The Bible teaches that the character of the Creator is loving and forgiving, a God who loves us during our good days and our bad days, who doesn't know how to do anything but *love*.

So how do we make ethical decisions that reflect the character of a loving God, of a servant Jesus?

> "The glory of God is a human being fully alive."
>
> St. Ireneus

How to Read the Bible : Session 4

Permission is granted to photocopy this handout for use with this session.

>>> **SESSION 5**

THE BIBLE SHAPES THE PEOPLE >>>
Translation as Interpretation

>>> **KEY VERSES**

First of all you must understand this, that no prophecy of scripture is a matter of one's own interpretation, because no prophecy ever came by human will, but men and women moved by the Holy Spirit spoke from God. (2 Peter 1:20-21)

>>> **FAITH STORY**

2 Peter 1:20-21; Acts 8:26-40

>>> **FAITH FOCUS**

Even the Bible writers interpreted scripture. In fact, there were real arguments about who interpreted correctly. In interpreting the Bible we will need to overcome two hurdles. The first is *translation*. The books of the Hebrew Bible were written in Hebrew and Aramaic and the New Testament in Greek, so they need to be translated for those of us who do not know the biblical languages. The other has to do with *interpretation*, with how we hear the message. Why do we not all hear or understand the same thing? How can we understand what the word of God is saying to us today?

>>> **SESSION GOAL**

Help participants experience interpretation as a community undertaking that shapes the people of God.

>>> **BIBLE STUDY SKILLS** to be practiced in this session: evaluate different Bible translations using Bible dictionaries and commentaries.

>>> **Materials needed and advance preparation**

- Copies of the handout for Session 5
- Find out what languages (besides English) your group knows or has studied (*Option A* in Focus)
- Paper and pencils
- Bibles, various translations, including NRSV
- Bible dictionaries
- One-volume Bible commentary, or commentaries on 1 Timothy
- Chalkboard/chalk or newsprint/marker

TEACHING PLAN

1. FOCUS 5 minutes

>>> **Option A:** If some members of your group know a language other than English, do a translation exercise. (**Note:** You must have at least **two** people who know the alternate language in common.)

1. Poll the group in advance to find out what languages they know or have studied.
2. Write this sentence (or choose your own) in English on one piece of paper:

   Reach for the stars: You might not get them, but you won't wind up with a handful of mud either.

   Write the same sentence in another language on a second paper, or use an Internet-based translator like BabelFish. **Note:** Make the sentence difficult enough so as to show the many possibilities the translator must weigh. If this is not possible, do it with two people prior to the meeting and bring the results to the group.
3. Give the papers to two people who each know the alternate language, and have them translate their sentence.

   Example: Person #1 translates the sentence from English to Spanish and person #2 translates it from Spanish to English.

   Compare the translations. Did any meanings change? If you like, exchange the translations and write a translation from the translation! Did the meanings change further from the original?

Continue with *Option A* under Connect.

>> **Option B:** Write "The Lord is my shepherd" (Psalm 23:1) on the board. Now ask each person to decide which word should be accented in the sentence. Notice that each time a different word is accented the meaning of the sentence changes! Point out how each person, by accenting a specific word, has already interpreted what the sentence means.

Continue with *Option B* under Connect.

2. CONNECT 5 minutes

>> **Option A:** Discuss the difficulties of translating from one language to another. How can you be sure you have translated correctly when there may be a number of different ways of translating?

>> **Option B:** Discuss the different meanings of the sentence, "The Lord is my shepherd." Why does the meaning change when you shift the accent? How do you know what the writer intended? Ask, *Which word **should** be accented in Psalm 23:1?* To find out we would have to read the rest of the psalm and notice that it talks about a shepherd leading sheep to green pastures. So we know that we should say, "The Lord is my **shepherd**."

Shift to the next activity by saying: *Even the biblical writers had to translate. Here's an example: Psalm 40:6 says, in Hebrew, the Lord has "given me an open ear." But when it is translated into Greek the writer of the book of Hebrews (10:5) says that the Lord has given him a body. Did the Greek translator take a mental holiday?*

3. EXPLORE THE BIBLE 5-15 minutes

Inform the group that in Hebrew "to hear" means to obey. In Greek obedience is expressed in terms of presenting your body! Then give the following mini-lecture about Bible translations:

Translations of the Bible
Explain that the Hebrew Bible, originally written in Hebrew, was already translated into Greek several centuries before the time of Christ. This translation, known as the Septuagint, contained more books than the Hebrew Bible (Old Testament). The early Christians probably used the Septuagint in their churches.

The New Testament books were written in Greek even though the Jews at that time spoke Aramaic. We have none of the original manuscripts of the biblical books. All we have are copies of copies.

We do, however, have translations of the Scriptures in over 2,000 languages. All of us work from such translations of the Bible.

Introduce the Bible story from Acts 8, and proceed either by reading the passage or setting up the "extra challenge option" outlined below:

Our story takes us to Acts 8:26-40. Here we find that a foreigner was trying to understand Isaiah 53, the passage about the suffering servant. We are not told which translation he had before him. Was it Greek? It could have been.

The Spirit of God told Philip to go meet this foreigner, who was a court official of the queen of Ethiopia. The Ethiopian must already have known something of the God of Israel, because he had come to Jerusalem to worship. Philip asked him if he understood what he was reading. The Ethiopian admitted he needed help in understanding the passage, so Philip interpreted the story for him.

Now compare Acts 8:32-33 with Isaiah 53:7-8. Talk about the differences. How would you explain them? Is anything said that would indicate that this refers to Jesus?

Comment as follows on the passage:

*The Ethiopian didn't need help because he was ignorant or uninformed. Even the scribes, the teachers of Judaism, had trouble knowing whether the passage referred to the suffering servant as a **person** who is to come, or to a whole **people**. In the four servant songs in Isaiah (Isaiah 42:1-9; 49:1-7; 50:4-11; 52:13–53:12) the servant is sometimes spoken of in the singular and sometimes in the plural. Finally, the scholars decided that it probably referred to a people, more particularly, to the people of Israel.*

But that is not how Philip interpreted the verse. He told the Ethiopian about Jesus the suffering servant of God; how Jesus was crucified for his obedience to God, but was raised by God from the dead. Philip pointed out to the Ethiopian how all these things happened in fulfillment of scripture and for our salvation. Philip's interpretation, while different from that of the Jewish scholars, inspired the Ethiopian to be baptized in the name of Jesus.

Extra challenge option (for studying the task of interpretation):
Do a dramatic reading of Acts 8:26-40. You'll need readers for:
- the angel
- the narrator
- the Spirit
- Philip
- the Ethiopian

Make sure you have the same translation of the Bible for all the readers. Assign parts and practice beforehand if possible.

4. APPLY 10-15 minutes

Hand out four different translations of the Bible, but **do not** bring attention to the fact that they are different. Then have four people read 1 Timothy 2:1-15 as a chorus.

When the babble and confusion die down, ask the rest of the group how much they understood. Chances are they won't have gotten much. Why? All the readers were reading the same verses! What's the difference?

>>> **LEGEND OF THE TRANSLATION OF THE SEPTUAGINT...**

has it that 72 Jewish scholars each worked separately to make a Hebrew-to-Greek translation of the Hebrew Scriptures. After 72 days they came together to compare the translations, and each one was the same in every way. While the legend may not be accurate in its detail, it was a way to emphasize that this translation was inspired by God. This became the Bible of the early Christians. Septuagint, by the way, is Greek for "seventy."

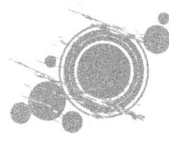

Then read each version separately. Are there differences in interpretation?

Now have everyone work together to write *one version* of the passage using the four translations. They can take pieces from each translation, or agree on one of the translations. Use Bible dictionaries and commentaries to help understand which words make the most sense to them, and still keep the best sense of the passage. They are to make a version that they feel is an interpretation that helps the faith community toward life and/or toward greater faithfulness. It may not be easy, but they may learn something about the task that translators face, and how interpretation of scripture is a corporate undertaking.

If they do not catch it, point out that the NRSV translates verses 1-7 as pertaining to both men and women, verse 8 to men, and verses 9-11 to women, the way it is in the Greek text. Bring the group an amplified version that shows the different possible translations of words.

5. RESPOND 5-10 minutes

Ask, *Which of the translations did you like best? Why?* Distribute the handout sheet that lists the differences between the most popular translations.

Next, have each person make a list of what they would look for when shopping for their own Bible, even if it is an app. What translation would they choose? (Some considerations might include: translator is individual or a group; beauty of language and poetry; in a language style that you easily understand; translation comes from the original Hebrew or Greek; a paraphrase.) What elements would they want included in their Bible? A study Bible? Concordance? Maps? Annotations?

Close with a prayer, asking God for wisdom in understanding the meaning of the Scriptures. Ask for God to be present whenever believers are working together to understand scripture. (**Note:** One of the options in the Extender Session pairs youth with adults to choose individual Bibles. It could function as a follow-up to this activity, and for closure to the unit.)

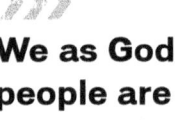

We as God's people are informed as well as formed by the story of God's coming in history.

INSIGHTS FROM SCRIPTURE

>> ### TRANSLATION

Languages are constantly changing. In order for the Bible to say the same thing it did in earlier generations, the translation has to be kept up to date because the old words no longer mean what they once did. Not only does the Bible have to be translated from the original language, but it has to be retranslated again and again. That is why we have so many translations even in English.

But which translation should we use? There is no easy solution. None is perfect. All have to make choices as to how to translate. Each will be better on some verses and not so good on other verses. As a general rule, one could advise that translations by single authors should be used more for private reading and study. For public reading and use we should use translations agreed to by a group of translators officially appointed by the church.

INTERPRETATION

Like language, our understanding of the Scriptures is not static. We grow in our knowledge and understanding, and add the wisdom of new text discoveries. This leads to more sensitive interpretation. We also build on the knowledge and understanding of those who have studied the Scriptures before us. We even gain in understanding through errors in interpretation that have been made in the past.

As cultures change and develop, new questions have to be asked. For example, there were no ethical questions about medical life support prior to the time that medical technology made it possible to keep the body alive even after the mind was dead. In the same way, new situations force us to bring new questions to the Scriptures.

But when new questions, new language, and new discoveries bring new interpretation, how do we decide on the *correct* interpretation? This is where the faith community comes in. It is always best to check our interpretation with others in the faith community.

Still the nagging question: How do we know the Bible isn't just a human expression passing itself off as divine? Bible scholar Etienne Charpentier (in *How to Read the Old Testament*) answers the question this way:

> "If the word of God had fallen in a pure state from heaven, we could do nothing but repeat it. If, however, it is the humble deciphering of human events by generations of believers, it continues to present itself to us in events of today. Reading the Bible perhaps invites us less to repeat what was discovered by our ancestors in the faith than to do what they did: to read the Word of God in our lives and in the life of the world."

In interpreting the Bible, we should be careful not to overlook the fact that it centers on God. We need to ask, "What does this passage tell us about the character of God?" Once we know the character of God, we will know the direction of history, the moral order, and the things that will lead to life. Knowing who God is will indicate who we are to be as persons created in God's image.

The Bible narrates for us God's relation to us as humans and to all creation. It tells the story of God's coming in history and in Jesus Christ. We as God's people are informed as well as formed by this story. As we make this story our own we will become more God-like and Christ-like in character. We will live into becoming God's people representing divine love in the world.

> **"Christ has no body but yours,**
> **No hands, no feet on earth but yours,**
> **Yours are the eyes with which he looks**
> **Compassion on this world,**
> **Yours are the feet with which he walks to do good,**
> **Yours are the hands, with which he blesses all the world.**
> **Yours are the hands, yours are the feet,**
> **Yours are the eyes, you are his body."**
>
> St. Teresa of Ávila (1515–1582)

An Incomplete Guide to Popular Bible Translations

Exploring tough questions facing youth today

NAB (New American Bible) • A commonly used Catholic translation, and the version used during Mass in the United States.

NRSV (New Revised Standard Version) • Update of the Revised Standard Version (RSV). National Council of Churches sponsored, with modern language that replaces masculine pronouns where both male and female are clearly intended. A semi-colloquial style written at grade 10 level (ages 16+). The Catholic edition of this translation is used during Mass in Canada.

GNT (Good News Translation, also known as Today's English Version) • Not for thorough study. This simpler translation is geared toward readers from age 12 and up. Available in a Catholic edition.

CEV (Contemporary English Version) • This translation is used in the *Lectionary for Masses with Children* in the United States. It is written for readers ages 10 and up.

NJB (New Jerusalem Bible) • Translated by Roman Catholic scholars.

The Message • Rendered in contemporary idiom, true to the tone, rhythm, and ideas, if not an original word-for-word conversion of Greek to English. By Eugene H. Peterson. Now available in a Catholic edition.

NLT (New Living Translation) • A newer, relatively simple translation. A new Catholic edition with an imprimatur is now available. Grade 6 level.

NIV (New International Version) • Completely new translation based on the most reliable manuscripts available. Not a revision of earlier versions. Written at a grade 7 level, by an interdenominational Protestant team of translators (1978).

KJV (King James Version) • First Protestant authorized (by King James I) version. Known for beauty of its language. Difficult to read in 17th-century English (published 1611), grade 12 level.

NKJV • Modern update of KJV. Traditional language without the "thee"s and "thou"s. Updated words, but choppy language since it retains the 17th-century sentence structure.

NASB (New American Standard Bible) • A respected formal translation, high on accuracy, based on Greek New Testament superior to the one available to the KJV translators. Often used as a study Bible. Grade 11 level.

Living Bible • Paraphrase that used the American Standard Bible as its text. Originally intended for personal devotion only. Sometimes presents debatable interpretation. Grade 8 level.

Permission is granted to photocopy this handout for use with this session.

››› EXTENDER SESSION
(best used after Session 5)

SO MANY CHOICES...

››› **Option A:** Bible-buying spree

››› SESSION GOAL
Enable youth to "own" their own study Bibles by having them choose the version they wish to purchase.

››› SESSION PLAN
Some in your group may have been given Bibles when they were in grade school. They're probably ready for a different kind of Bible now, one with study aids that will help them dig deeper. Help youth to "own" their Bibles by pairing them up with adults who will shop with them for a study Bible. Perhaps you can get your congregation to foot the bill. The pairs could set their own times to make the trip, or get together to do it. Another option is to shop together through a website. However, consider the value of supporting a local, rather than a chain, bookstore.

Feel free, however, to go on the Bible-buying spree *before* you start the unit, if you want your youth to learn by using their own Bibles throughout this study. If you do this, discuss the issue of translation (borrow material from Session 5) before you do the shopping.

››› **Option B:** View and discuss the iconic film/play *Fiddler on the Roof* to get a feel for the power of tradition (remembering the past) in Hebrew/Jewish culture.

In Real Life
Exploring tough questions facing youth today

CLUELESS AND CALLED
Discipleship and the Gospel of Mark

What does it take to be a disciple? This study of the Gospel of Mark focuses on the requirements for following Jesus' way and the abundant life that is ours as a result. (5 sessions)

DO MIRACLES HAPPEN?
Signs and Wonders in the Gospel of John

The greatest miracle, recorded in John 1:14 and 3:16, is the miracle of God's love that became flesh and lived among us. But John also included examples of what we more traditionally think of as miracles: the wonder of abundance from little; healing; signs of impossibility and faith; and the resurrection. (5 sessions)

DO THE RIGHT THING
Ethics Shaped by Faith

How do you know what's right and what's wrong? Even when you figure it out, the right thing is often the unpopular or unpleasant choice. This unit offers participants a clearer sense of what it means to claim a faith identity, a foundation that can help them sort out the gritty details of ethics shaped by faith. (6 sessions)

FIGHT RIGHT
A Christian Approach to Conflict Resolution

This unit will help youth understand conflict and its function. They will learn how they can be honest and loving, and explore how conflict can be used for positive results. They will also learn ways to enhance their communication skills. 1 Corinthians. (5 sessions)

GOD IS A WARRIOR?
Violence in the Bible

The Bible challenges us to be reconciled to one another and work for justice. So what do we do with the stories that seem to condone violence or even encourage it? A discussion of issues in the Old and New Testaments. (6 sessions)

HOW DO YOU KNOW?
Wisdom in the Bible

Wisdom literature teaches us that we gain knowledge of the world, ourselves, and God through experience and observation. This unit provides practical, hands-on wisdom to help young people avoid life's snares and grow closer to God. Proverbs, Job, Ecclesiastes. (5 sessions)

HOW TO BE A TRUE FRIEND
The Bible Reveals Friendship's Heart

To be a friend takes skill. Help youth discover the secrets of friendship through various stories from the Old and New Testament. (6 sessions)

HOW TO READ THE BIBLE
Building Skills for Bible Study

What kind of book is the Bible? What does this book mean to me? This unit looks at the Bible as revelation, as history, as literature. Selected scripture. (5 sessions)

KEEPING THE GARDEN
A Faith Response to God's Creation

If Christians believe that God made the world, we do not need any more compelling reason to care for it than that God has handed us a treasure to hold and protect. This unit gets beyond trendy environmentalism and challenges youth to see environmental awareness as a religious issue. Genesis. (6 sessions)

MANTRAS, MENORAHS, AND MINARETS
Encountering Other Faiths

How is Christianity different from other faiths? Why do others believe the way they do? This study can give youth a new appreciation for the uniqueness of Jesus. Selected scripture. (5 sessions)

SALT, LIGHT, AND THE GOOD LIFE
The Beatitudes and the Sermon on the Mount

What can youth expect in a life of discipleship? This unit explores the Sermon on the Mount under four main sections: the Beatitudes, Salt and Light, Jesus and the Law, and Heavenly Teachings. Matthew 5. (6 sessions)

A SPECK IN THE UNIVERSE
The Bible on Self-Esteem and Peer Pressure

Discover God's unconditional love and acceptance of all people. This study will show positive ways to have one's life make a difference, and help youth find ways to resist negative peer pressure and turn it into positive action. (6 sessions)

THE RADICAL REIGN
Parables of Jesus

Jesus used parables to reveal what the kingdom of God is like, and how God relates to us. This study highlights how the parables reveal God's reign as radically different from the world we live in, and what that means for the Christian life. (6 sessions)

TESTING THE WATERS
Basic Tenets of Faith

Discover the biblical roots for the central Christian concepts of covenant, community, and baptism. This short course is a way to test the (baptismal) waters of Christianity before diving in, or review the basics for those who already have. (6 sessions)

WHO IS GOD?
Engaging the Mystery

God is beyond human comprehension, yet desires to be known. These sessions focus on the way we get clues about and glimpses of God from the Bible, God's creation, and church tradition. Selected scripture. (5 sessions)